T. J.

I LOOK FORWARD TO
THE POSSIBILITY OF
WORKING WITH YOU & THIS
KPMG TEAM!

Best,

Kevin

GET WHAT YOU WANT
BY SAYING WHAT YOU MEAN.

MAKE YOUR POINT

SPEAK CLEARLY
AND CONCISELY
ANYPLACE,
ANYTIME.

BOB ELLIOTT   KEVIN CARROLL

authorHOUSE™

1663 LIBERTY DRIVE, SUITE 200
BLOOMINGTON, INDIANA 47403
(800) 839-8640
WWW.AUTHORHOUSE.COM

First published by AuthorHouse 01/01/05

ISBN: 1-4208-0439-1 (sc)
ISBN: 1-4208-0440-5 (dj)

Printed in the United States of America
Bloomington, Indiana

This book is printed on acid-free paper.

ACKNOWLEDGEMENTS

Both of us originally worked for much larger organizations. So, our thanks to all of our former colleagues who encouraged us to go out on our own to pursue entrepreneurial enterprises…and to a few ex-bosses who did likewise for other reasons.

Next, we want to thank the thousands of clients we have worked with over the past twenty years. We have learned something new every time we've coached. Our seminars and workshops have been opportunities for us to hone our skills. They also acted as laboratories to introduce new techniques and continue to prove theories. As Yogi Berra put it: "You can observe a lot by watching." So, thank you clients for helping us improve daily.

While about a dozen talented friends and clients have read various drafts of the book and added to its content, three people deserve special mention. First, Mike Leach, a publisher and author of five books, was our trusty guide and advisor throughout the entire process of writing and editing. Judith Eckles, President of a communications firm bearing her own name, read and edited the last two drafts catching mistakes and adding great value. And, Bob Tayler, a talented designer, worked with us on the cover design and chapter layouts helping us through several iterations. Three cheers for Mike, Judith and Bob.

And finally, thanks to our families for their encouragement and support, especially to our wives, Elise and Mary, two women who are *very* skilled at making their point.

MAKE YOUR POINT!

TABLE OF CONTENTS

DELIVERY

HANDLING Q & A

THE WRAP-UP

INTRODUCTION

How this book will help you

True story #1: A young man, the Director of Public Relations for a big firm, ran into the new CEO on an elevator. The CEO said "What's new?" After six floors of "uh, uh, uh," the CEO got off the elevator and walked away with an unfavorable first impression of the man.

True story #2: The Marketing VP of a consumer packaged-goods company started her presentation with a laundry list of *fifteen* new programs and then presented them to a completely disinterested audience who gave up concentrating after the first few ideas.

True story #3: A top engineer apologized for the technical detail of his presentation and then proceeded to show a bunch of PowerPoint slides incorporating 300 data points in each. Too bad for him that he didn't realize that an audience can't read an "eye chart" and listen to the presenter at the same time.

You talk with people all day long. But do you leave them wondering… What's his point? What's she trying to say? Why should I care? What am I supposed to do?

You're always communicating…on the phone, in an elevator, in front of your boss, or in front of a throng of people. Every time you have the opportunity to speak, you have the obligation to speak clearly and concisely to make your point. How good are you at painting a logical and understandable picture that is orderly as well as interesting? When people listen to you, do they hear a leader?

People who can't communicate in business don't succeed. It's as simple as that. If you can't make your point, someone else will. But when you *can* communicate effectively, you project a much more favorable image: people listen to you, you're more influential, you have less stress, you gain more respect, and ultimately, you're more successful.

Social scientists tell us that people are more likely to comprehend and remember messages that are limited in number, repeated, reinforced and supported with interesting evidence. In this book, we will share with you a simple and unique model that we call *THE DIAMOND*. As you will discover, *THE DIAMOND* is a great tool that will help you develop and deliver your message to any audience of any length whether you're in an auditorium, on a conference call, hosting a webcast or even leaving a voicemail. *THE DIAMOND* will sharpen your communication skills immediately.

Make Your Point! was written to help businessmen and women who are smart, honest and hard-working, but feel that they don't present themselves or their ideas as well as they could because either they have a hard time building a logical argument or they don't project confidence.

This is an uncomplicated book about uncomplicating your personal and business communications. It's about organizing, honing and delivering your messages whether they're given formally or informally. We had fun writing *Make Your Point!* We hope you enjoy reading it.

SECTION ONE

PREPARATION

CHAPTER ONE

YOU'RE ALWAYS ON STAGE

ANTICIPATE THE CONVERSATION.

A number of years ago, the receptionist at an ad agency where a friend of ours worked was about to retire. To celebrate her transition, the staff threw a little office party in her honor. As everyone was milling around in the lobby making small talk and enjoying a cocktail, a couple of people came up to our friend and said, "We're about to bring the cake out now and we thought it would be nice if you gave a little toast." Seconds later about fifty coworkers were staring at him awaiting his words. Our friend paused. He stammered. He paused again. He told a lame story. He bombed.

It didn't have to be that way. Had our pal taken a few minutes before the party to prepare his thoughts just in case he might be asked to say something, he could've given the receptionist the sendoff she deserved.

We're always on stage. Whether in an elevator, walking down the hall, on a conference call or at the podium, we should always be prepared to make our point.

Of course, the more formal the occasion, the more time you'll want to spend preparing your thoughts. However, there are countless informal times where you'll be put on the spot. Trust us, you'll wish you had taken a few moments beforehand to gather your ideas.

In the case of the retirement speech that was sprung on our friend, it wouldn't have taken much time to get ready. With five minutes prep time, he could have easily come up with a funny story. Or he could have found an inspiring quote. Or he could have jotted down

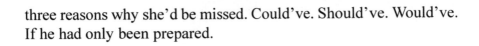

three reasons why she'd be missed. Could've. Should've. Would've. If he had only been prepared.

◇

CHAPTER TWO

A WORD ABOUT SIMPLICITY

SIMPLICITY BEATS COMPLEXITY.

We are bombarded with messages.

Do you have any idea how many ads Mr. and Ms. Average American are exposed to in one day? About 2,500 give or take a few hundred. 2,500! That means that if we're awake an average of 16 hours a day, that's over 150 ads an hour (this includes TV, radio, the internet, outdoor advertising, and the like).

Add to that all the non-commercial messages such as newspaper articles, TV shows, radio programs, magazine pieces, phone calls, emails, letters, bills, memos, post it notes, refrigerator magnets, yada, yada, yada. It's clear that our brains are under assault. And unfortunately for you, that cacophony of communication is what you're up against when *you're* trying to make *your* point.

So how are you going to break through the clutter to help make certain your message gets through?

Simplicity. Knowing what you want to say and saying it simply.

Please don't let your lack of preparation or your own insecurities compel you to say more than you have to. More information doesn't mean better information. The Gettysburg Address had only 261 words. Contrast that to a recent *New York Times* article referring to a Presidential candidate saying: "(He) has been talking for years, and yet such is the thicket of his verbiage that he has achieved almost complete strategic ambiguity."

The average person you talk to has the attention span of a gnat (your authors included). Keep your message simple and you'll have a better chance of getting it to stick.

Here's a fun brainteaser we found: How would you simplify this sentence? *Visible vapors that issue from carbonaceous materials are a harbinger of imminent conflagration.* Hint: it's a common proverb. (You'll find the answer at the end of the last chapter.)

CHAPTER THREE

YOU ARE YOUR BRAND
A WALKING, TALKING PRODUCT

Just like your neighbor Alice, who buys Wisk® laundry detergent because it's the brand she has come to know and trust, your "consumers" (your boss, co-workers, clients, prospects, friends) are more or less likely to buy into what you have to say based on the image they have of you. Are you doing all you can to project your most favorable "brand" image?

Not only are you the brand itself, you're also the brand's product manager. And just like the product managers for Skippy®, Cheerios®, or Becks®, you're in charge of your product, packaging, advertising and promotion.

Your *product* is the content of your message. It's the verbal message you're trying to get across.

Your *packaging* is your non-verbal communications. Not only how you dress, but how you energize your message as you speak – confidently, clearly and with conviction.

Your *advertising* is how you deliver your message so it sticks. Television commercials try to grab you, stay with a single theme and concisely outline the benefits. So should you.

Your *promotion* for the product is your planned communications exposure with an appeal. For you, it's being up to the task of clearly and concisely telling your message anyplace, anytime.

In the chapters ahead, we will show you ways to improve both what you say *and* how you say it. Apply these concepts and just watch how your consumers respond.

CHAPTER FOUR

SEIZE THE MOMENT

BE WILLING TO SPEAK UP.

The New Yorker heralded Noam Chomsky of M.I.T as "one of the greatest minds of the twentieth century." The magazine, however, also said that Chomsky had "a voice so quiet that, unless he has a microphone, it is difficult to hear him." They added, "He gives his words so little force that they scarcely leave his mouth."

If we all had as much brain power as Mr. Chomsky, we could easily suffer through these vocal shortcomings. But for those of us that don't hang out in that stratosphere of intelligence, we'd better make an effort to be heard...to raise our voices and increase the regularity of communicating our messages. In short, we need to seize the moment and be heard.

All of us know people that are too aggressive: the loudmouth, the bragger, and the overly ambitious. "He's so brash." "She's so pushy." "I can't get a word in edgewise." But we also know the "shrinking violets" who suffer from benign aloofness. "He's so withdrawn that I never know what he's thinking." Or, "I know she's very bright, but why doesn't she say something?" Successful communicators are those who know when to speak, and who look for opportunities to make their point.

Many of us simply need to pick up our energy level, annunciate our words, and add power to our thoughts. Performance counts. Being prepared with convincing messages to be delivered either spontaneously or formally takes discipline. Take the time to know what messages you want to have ready to deliver at any time. And then organize your messages into bite-sized pieces so you can serve them up whenever necessary.

Remember the tribulations of George W. Bush in his early speeches? Pundits said that "George Bush's lips are where words go to die." Don't kill words, thoughts and messages.

It is organically impossible and wouldn't be a good idea to change who you are...your speaking style, personality and thinking processes. But it's not impossible to enhance all of these by developing a more forceful and ambitious speaking capability.

If you don't tell your story, someone else will...and it won't often be the story you want told.

Chapter Five

ARE YOU TALKING TO ME?
Know your audience.

A major technology firm once hired us to sit in on a number of briefings they were going to give to some prospective customers. In a sense, they wanted us to be the proverbial fly on the wall. The client sensed that they could improve how they conducted these very important meetings and wanted our guidance.

In one briefing, a researcher from the technology company stood up and gave a presentation about Java (for those of you who don't speak geek, Java is a type of computer programming language). The presenter went into great depth about all sorts of minutia about Java such as creating a GUI with JFC/Swing and writing applets. Egad! About 20 minutes into the presentation, one of the prospective customers raised his hand and said: "What's Java?" Unfortunately for the researcher, that prospect felt buried under a boatload of irrelevant information. Had the researcher taken the time *beforehand* to consider how much knowledge the audience had and what was important (and not important) to them, that wouldn't have happened. Remember, it's not just about what *you* want to tell them, it's also about what *they* want to know.

Similar to the above, a friend of ours who has a seven-year-old daughter who plays softball, shared a story with us. He told us that his daughter's team was in the field and the other team was at bat. With all good intentions, one of his daughter's coaches yelled out to the girls: "Force on Second. Force on second." WHAT?! Force on Second? What the heck does "force on second" mean to a seven-year-old? Evidently that coach didn't consider his audience and he was destined to be yet another unsuccessful communicator. He should've thought more about who he was talking to and said something like: "Girls, if the ball is hit to you, throw it to Claire on second base."

The same thing is true in business. Before making your point, *always* consider who you're talking to. Here are some of the most critical questions you must consider:

- Who is in my audience? (Demographics: age, sex, education, etc.)
- How much do they know about my subject?
- What is their attitude about me, my department, my company and my subject?
- What issues are important and not important to them?
- What is *their* objective? (Why are they here?)
- What can I say that will be of value to them?
- How much time do they have?

You may have come up with a sophisticated new anti-friction braking system that cuts down gas consumption, noise pollution, g-forces and lots of other nifty things that *you* love talking about, but if your listeners are more interested in the color of the car, they're going to tune you out.

If you want to become a better communicator and be more persuasive, you need to really know your target so that you can adapt your message accordingly. As we said before, it's not about what you want to tell them, it's about what they want to know.

CHAPTER SIX

WIIFM

WHAT'S IN IT FOR ME?

WIIFM stands for *What's in it for me?* Essentially, it's what most everyone you talk to wants to know. Since humans generally act in their own self-interest (we're writing this book for fame and fortune) they want to know: What's in it for me? What will I get out of this? Why should I do what you're asking me to do? If you can clearly show them what's in it for them, you'll be a lot more persuasive.

At The Bronx Zoo in New York City, there's an exhibit called The World of Darkness. Inside it's pitch black and houses nocturnal creatures such as raccoons, skunks, and bats. Years ago, on the line to go into the exhibit, there was a sign that stated: "Please do not run or scream while in the World of Darkness or you will frighten the animals." That's pretty clear, right? But the problem was that people were still running and screaming. Why do you suppose that was? Because the sign was missing something! It was missing WIIFM. The Bronx Zoo hadn't given visitors any compelling reason not to run or scream.

Eventually a second sign had to be added below the first sign. The second sign read: "If you frighten the animals, they will hide and *you will not be able to see them.*" Now that's WIIFM!

The most effective communicators first consider *who* they're speaking to and then they make a point of telling their listener how the listener will *benefit* from what they have to say. Some of the most common WIIFM's are: you'll make more money, you'll be less stressed, you'll be more productive, you'll lose weight, you'll be happier, you'll be more successful, you'll gain more respect, etc. You get the idea.

One more anecdote to show that the opportunity to apply WIIFM is around us all the time…a friend of ours wanted his young daughter to get her hair trimmed because he felt it was getting too long and didn't look that good on her. One day, when they were out driving around, he suggested they visit the hair stylist. But his daughter didn't want to. He asked again, but this time he told her that he thought she would look better with a haircut (that was his need), but again she declined. Finally, knowing his daughter, he considered why *she* might want to get her hair cut and he came up with a new approach: "Honey, if you get your hair cut, it will take a lot less time to dry it." Her response? "Okay, Daddy."

CHAPTER SEVEN

KNOW WHERE YOU'RE GOING

WHAT'S YOUR OBJECTIVE?

Imagine you're going on vacation. You've packed up your spouse and kids, you're on the road, you even beat the traffic, but you haven't decided where you're going yet. Doesn't make sense, does it?

As Yogi Berra once said, "If you don't know where you're going, you might end up someplace else." It's the same way when we communicate with others. Pleeeeease don't start talking unless you have a clear idea in your head what you're trying to say. Sounds obvious doesn't it? But the truth is that plenty of us start talking before we know exactly what we're thinking. It becomes difficult to make your point when you're not quite sure what your point is.

One of the most important questions you should ask yourself is: Is my objective to simply *inform* my listener, or is my objective to *persuade* them to do something? In all the years we've coached people, it seems to us that many people take the easy way out and they decide that their objective is to just give information when really what they needed to do was to persuade. Know what you're trying to say and, whenever possible, frame it as a persuasive discussion rather than just another information download.

Let's say, for example, that you think your objective is "To update (inform) my team leader on xyz project." Well that may be fine, but does your team leader really care about an update? What is the *underlying purpose* of the update? What *value* does the update have to your team leader? You'd do better to frame your objective as: "To convince (persuade) my team leader that we are on time and on budget for xyz project."

Have a specific purpose.

SECTION
TWO

CONTENT

MAKE YOUR POINT!

CHAPTER EIGHT

LOGIC RULES

HAVE A BEGINNING, MIDDLE AND END.

Have you ever flipped through one of those children's quiz books where they show a comic strip, but the individual frames are all out of order? The challenge is to put the frames back into a logical sequence so that the comic strip makes sense. There are lots of combinations that you could make, but only one is the most reasonable.

Clarity and comprehension will result from the flow of your thoughts and the order you put them in. Your listener's brain may be tired or overloaded, but it always seeks logic. When you speak, you must provide your listener with a *logical* argument. Everything should be in its proper place.

If you've ever had presentation training, you know that nearly all communication coaches will outline a sequence for a good presentation as follows: "Tell them what you're going to tell them (the beginning)…tell them (the middle)…and then tell them what you just told them (the end)." Great advice. Otherwise, a listener's attention will wane if you don't lay out a logical sequence. Don't complicate your message by creating detours in your logic roadmap.

In any message delivery, you're there for a reason…to make a program understandable, to create action, to justify your job or to sell a product or an idea. And your audience is there for a reason, too. They're there to either understand something, to do something or to buy something. Your job is to bring those two objectives as close together as possible. When you have a commonsense sequence, you will be more successful.

Whether it's the thirty second "stop by" message, the five-minute staff meeting report or the forty-five minute conference presentation, comprehensible communication needs a beginning, middle and end. As you'll see in the next chapter on THE DIAMOND, you need to state your main topic upfront, develop the sub-topics in the body of your presentations, and then state your conclusion at the end. This is the way people comprehend things.

Chapter Nine

THIS DIAMOND IS A GEM

Organizing your content

Why do so many speakers wander aimlessly through their presentations thinking that their audience really wants to work that hard to try to follow them? Don't they realize that it's not the job of the listener to do all of the work; it's the job of the speaker? It's the listener's job to *absorb* the information, not decipher it.

As we said in the previous chapter, your listeners will better comprehend your ideas when you present them logically. As communicators, we need to clearly state what our idea is, back it up with evidence, and color it with interesting, provocative concepts.

And so THE DIAMOND model that you see throughout this section of the book was created by your authors. It incorporates the need for order...a beginning, middle and end and the concept of three sub-topics (max) in the main body of your presentation.

Here's how THE DIAMOND works:

First, you need to grab your listener's attention. Without the *attention* of an audience, you don't have an audience. Establish rapport. Tell a personal story, ask a question, throw out a surprising statistic, or use some other device to connect you with your audience.

Then, right up front, clearly and concisely state your *main topic*. Don't keep anyone guessing. Tell them what they are going to hear and tell them why they should care. (Remember, they want to know *what's in it for me?*)

Next, you should give a very brief *preview* of your three sub-topics. The entire content of your presentation will be wrapped up in these three conceptual ideas. By the way, when you deliver your previews, clearly say: "Number one, Number two and Number three." If you don't, your audience won't be able to track with you easily.

After your brief preview, you need to develop each of the *three sub-topics* within the "body" of your presentation. Each of the three sub-topics will have supporting evidence to substantiate it. This is the meat of your message.

After you finish your third sub-topic, each of the three sub-topics then needs to be briefly *summarized* so that your audience can refocus on the three key ideas. Again, you will want to say "Number one, number two and number three" so that your audience stays in sync with you.

Then comes the *conclusion,* which is a restatement of the "so what?" of the entire presentation that you gave in the beginning. Again, tell them why they should care about what you just talked about. Relate it to them.

And, finally, the appeal or *action* step. This is where you tell your listeners what you want them to do as a next step. Don't just leave them hanging.

Every listener wants to know where you are, where you are going, and where you reach resolution. So follow THE DIAMOND and it will help you package your message in a clear, concise way. The following chapters will each highlight one section of THE DIAMOND followed by an example of how all the pieces work together.

THE DIAMOND
A Simple Design for Organizing Your Content

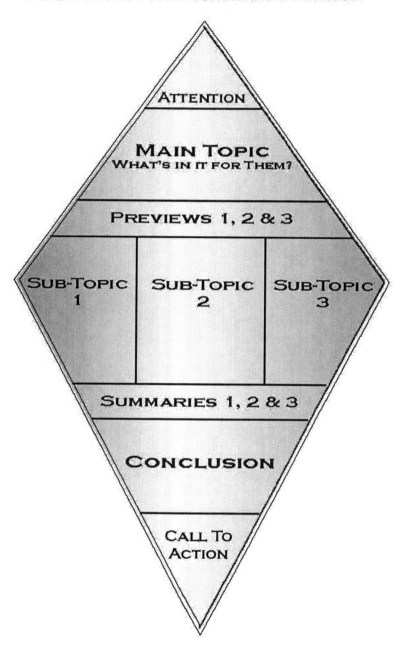

Attention

Main Topic
What's in it for Them?

Previews 1, 2 & 3

Sub-Topic 1 | Sub-Topic 2 | Sub-Topic 3

Summaries 1, 2 & 3

Conclusion

Call To Action

And one more thing...THE DIAMOND isn't just for formal presentations. It can be used easily to help you make your point on phone calls, webcasts, emails, voicemails and in informal elevator conversations when the boss says: "So what's going on with Project Whatchamacallit?"

CHAPTER TEN

SET THE BAIT

HAVE AN ATTENTION GETTER.

Recently we saw a motivational speaker walk to the front of the room, stand before his audience, pull out a camera and take their photo. Within an instant, he had their attention. His audience was surprised and intrigued. About ten minutes into his speech, he revealed that he had recently suffered a unique illness that had severely affected his short term memory. The reason he had taken the audience's photo was because it would be his only memory of speaking to them!

In the world of marketing and advertising, there's a well-known acronym called AIDA. It stands for Attention, Interest, Desire, Action. AIDA is the golden path to persuasion.

If your ultimate objective is to get someone to do something (action), you have to start by first grabbing their attention. The same thing holds true when you talk to people. In order to make your point, the first thing you have to do is grab their attention. If you don't hook 'em early, you'll lose 'em early.

So how do you grab someone's attention? Well you can start by using a creative device such as a personal story, analogy or surprising statistic and *link* it to the subject you're talking about. For example, if you want to talk about goal setting, you might read an excerpt from a magazine article about someone who accomplished an amazing feat. If you want to talk about improving productivity, ask your listeners to guess how long it took to build the Empire State Building (13 months!). If you want to talk about getting spending under control, you might start by burning a dollar bill. (Okay, so it's

THE DIAMOND

STEP 1 - GRAB THEIR ATTENTION

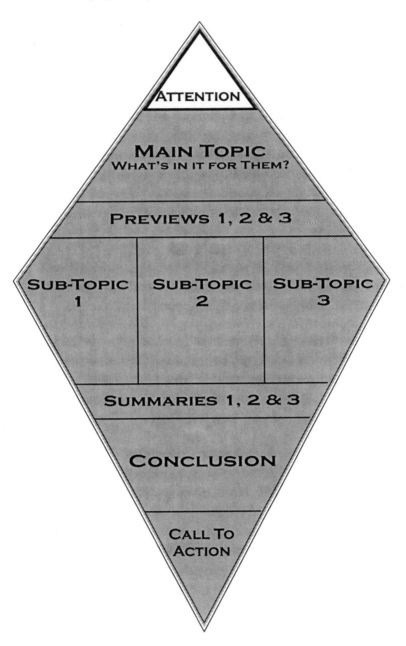

illegal to burn money and you might set off a fire alarm, but you get the idea.)

Next time you watch TV, take a look at the commercials and keep an eye out for all the different methods that are used to hook the viewer and make the product or service memorable. You'll see how the pros grab our attention. You can do the same.

Finally, attention getters shouldn't be limited to just your opening. Sprinkle in attention getters (we sometimes call these "sizzle") along the way in order to keep your listener engaged.

CHAPTER ELEVEN

NO DOUBT ABOUT IT

CLEARLY ESTABLISH YOUR MAIN TOPIC.

Getting the attention of an audience or listener is critical. But what happens after that? How can you maintain that attention and spell out, without any doubt, your reason for talking to them? It's called the Main Topic or the "here" and "hear"…why I'm here and what you'll be hearing about.

When you get to know THE DIAMOND model, you'll know that, while the main topic precedes the three sub-topics, the main topic is really an umbrella for all three sub-topics. Let's say your three sub-topics are: "One, experience pays off…it's all about our people. Two, you shouldn't be looking for products…look for solutions. And three, old technologies don't work…we invest in new technologies." Then your main topic statement that covers these three ideas could be something like: "We're here today to tell you about our company and its capabilities. More importantly, we believe that the difference between adequate value and exceptional value is locked in what a company really stands for. We measure our success in three core philosophies..." And then go on to your three sub-topics.

The main topic must leave no doubt as to why you're commanding the time of an audience. Otherwise, you're in the wrong place at the wrong time. It's amazing to us how often we see smart people jump right into the sub-topics of their presentation without first establishing what the overall purpose (main topic) of their presentation is. If you're trying to get someone's approval to invest $100,000 in a research study, then state that right up front. Don't leave them guessing as to what your main purpose is.

THE DIAMOND
STEP 2 - ESTABLISH YOUR MAIN TOPIC

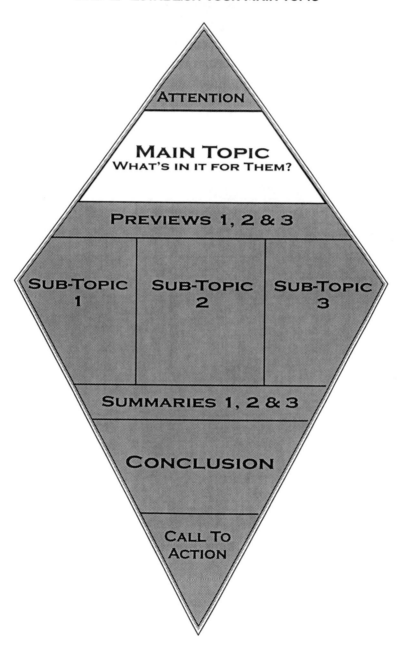

Also included with the main topic should be your WIIFM statement. State clearly and concisely right up front what's in it for your listener. What benefit(s) will they get from listening to you or from doing what you're asking them to do? If you can save them time, tell them. If you can help them make more sales, tell them. If you can help them lower inventory costs, tell them. Never assume that the benefit is obvious; you need to tell them!

CHAPTER TWELVE

THE MAGIC OF 3'S

WHY THREE SUB-TOPICS IS THE PERFECT NUMBER

We think in a world of threes: Small, medium, large. Morning, noon, night. The three act play. Past, present, future. The three stooges. Fours, fives and sixes clutter the mind and are too many things to remember, while two just doesn't seem to be quite enough.

THE DIAMOND model demands that the presenter organize every bit of information and content around *three* sub-topics. Some people argue that they really need to present a minimum of five ideas or complain that they can't arrive at more than two sub-topics. With a little thought, everyone can find a way to take their subject matter and come up with *three* good sub-topics that fully cover it.

As you'll see from the diagram in this chapter, the preview portion of your presentation comes *after* your main topic and is simply the place where you *briefly* mention what your three sub-topics will be. You don't want to go into any depth at this point.

The preview portion of a capabilities presentation for a company could talk about: One, its unwavering commitment to technology… two, the wealth of talent in the organization…and three, its history of leadership in the industry. Or someone selling a new training program might organize a talk around: One, the proven success of programs like this in the past…two, the cost-effectiveness of the program…and three, the promising results of the testing done in the field.

Series of 3's just work. Here's a series of six things: bread, beans, beer, bacon, baloney and butter. Quick…what are the six things? Isn't it easier to remember three: bread, beans and beer?

Want to present a new product idea? Your three sub-topics could be: One, the reason for the new product…two, the investment behind the new product…and finally, three, the product's proven reliability. Sure, you could make six, seven or eight separate points about the product, but hold back. Find a way to fold those additional points under your three core sub-topics.

In many of our workshops, as a way to practice the use of 3's, we ask participants to structure a talk around a non-business subject; we call this exercise *Instant Expert*. Two subjects we often use: 1) Preparing for a bird calling contest and 2) Making chicken soup. On the bird calling contest, the three sub-topics might be: One, observe the bird. Two, call the bird. And three, be the bird. (Once a client put a cracker half-way into his mouth and went over to a colleague and started feeding the cracker to him just like a mother bird feeds her chicks. Now that's how you "be the bird.")

In a presentation on making chicken soup, someone might focus on: One, the different varieties of chicken soup (with rice, noodles, plain broth, vegetables, etc.). Two, the importance of a fresh kosher chicken. And three, how to season the soup.

One, two, three.

Try to think and present in 3's. It's more memorable, it parallels the way other people think and it's easy to organize. (Gee, that's three things.)

And remember…when you say your three sub-topics in your preview, in your body and in you summary, make certain you *say* the numbers "one, two, three" or "first, second, third" *each* time. If you don't, your audience will be more likely to get lost. (We've seen this happen plenty of times.)

THE DIAMOND

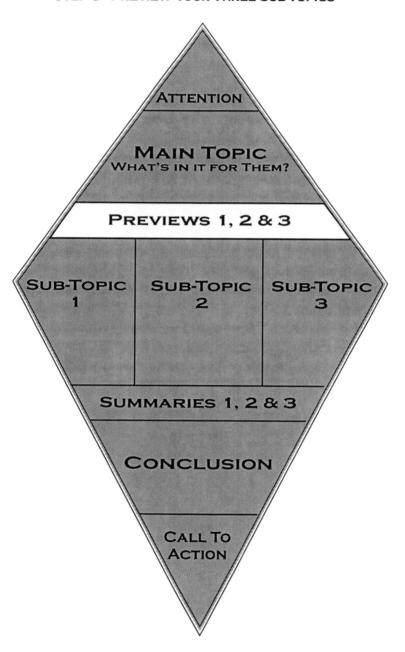

CHAPTER THIRTEEN

MAKE IT STICK

MAKE YOUR THREE SUB-TOPICS MEMORABLE.

When you decide on the three sub-topics that will be the three legs of your "communication stool," give some thought to how you're going to really make the topics *stick* with your listener. If you don't, you risk the chance that your message will get lost in the barrage of other messages of the day. Luckily for you, the overwhelming majority of people will err on the boring side…they play it safe. So it won't take much for you to stand above the crowd.

Get your creative juices going and figure out an intriguing way to take expected topics and turn them into the unexpected. For example, here are three expected topics that one might come up with to talk about a new widget: 1) The Benefits 2) The Drawbacks 3) The Biggest Obstacles. There's nothing wrong with this, however with a little creativity, you might come up with: 1) The Good 2) The Bad 3) The Ugly. Listeners will remember The Good, The Bad and The Ugly. And they'll remember you. (No, we're not suggesting you're ugly.)

CHAPTER FOURTEEN

THE EVIDENCE PLEASE

SUPPORT AND PROVE YOUR ASSERTIONS

"This product will really do the job." Oh really? How? "Our group is the top group in the organization." OK...prove it. "We're not going to make our numbers this quarter." Why not? If you're going to make your point, you need to support any and all claims in your sub-topics with evidence for those claims. One or two of the following will usually do the trick: statistics, anecdotes, stories, examples, third-party opinion or personal experience.

The presentations you make, whether formal or informal, long or short, are laced with assertions. Assertions are the life-blood of communication. "I can do the job." "This program is sensational." "We're going to increase profits." "We really know your industry." And on and on. But why in the world would anyone believe these hollow claims, unless you provide the facts (evidence) to support them?

So when you make assertions in the body of your presentation, construct "proof points" that provide the evidence for those assertions. This is what will make up the substance of your sub-topics.

First, examples. Don't just tell me that you have experience in my industry. Back it up. Cite examples of programs you've run and specific experiences you've had. Statistics are next. Use numbers as proof points. Don't say "We do a lot in that marketplace." Say, "We have a 62% market share." By the way, numbers can be overwhelming and sometimes deceptive. Use them judiciously. And, please, for you number crunchers who like to talk about billions of dollars, put the numbers into perspective. Did you know that a billion hours ago, nothing stood on this earth on two legs?

Analogies are also points of evidence. A client of ours, the head of a micro-brewery, was being criticized because much of his "micro-brewed beer" was being produced on contract by major national brewers. So he repositioned the criticism by saying: "If the great cook Julia Child came to your house with her ingredients and her recipes, but cooked dinner for you in your kitchen, isn't that still a Julia Child meal?" Good analogy.

Stories. Most stories are tales about interesting, sometimes humorous incidents. Presenting is storytelling and the more anecdotes you can include within the big story, the more convincing you'll be.

Third-party opinion is another proof point method. Let someone else tell the story. Quote customers, consultants to the industry, or anyone with credibility. Sometimes quoting the media can be effective, too.

And, finally, your own personal experience. Most of us are a bit reluctant to toot our own horns, but there is nothing more powerful than the person who says "Look. I've been in this industry for 30 years. I've seen four business cycles and a complete overhaul of manufacturing processes. Yet, we have grown over this time on average 25% a year."

Be your own "assertions cop." Don't let your claims go unsupported.

THE DIAMOND
STEP 4 - DELIVER YOUR THREE SUB-TOPICS

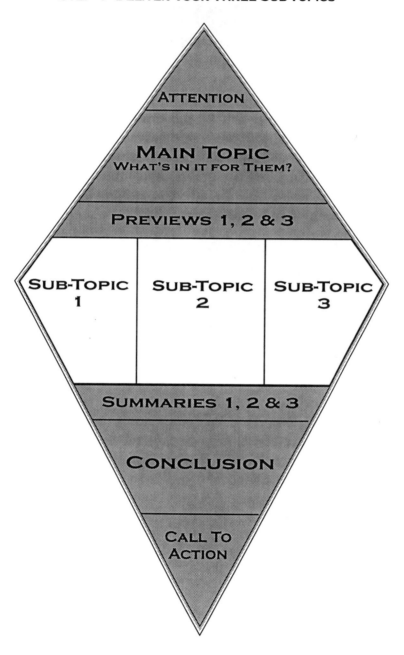

CHAPTER FIFTEEN

TO SUM IT UP

TELL THEM WHAT YOU TOLD THEM.

So you've just given a wonderful presentation using THE DIAMOND model. You gained the audience's attention, effectively stated the topic, previewed your three provocative sub-topics and have fully explained and supported your three sub-topics. Boy, do you feel good. You're like a horse at the end of the ride rushing back to the barn. Well not quite. You still have to provide an effective *summary* for each of your three ideas.

Let's say you're doing a capabilities presentation on your company. If you truly want everyone in the audience to remember your three points, you must recap and say something like: "Now let me summarize. First, there is our important investment in technology; a full 21% of annual revenue goes into IT. My second point is the depth of knowledge and experience of our people...the average employee has fourteen years in our industry. And, my third point is our size...we have thirty two percent of the total market."

Our point is this: at the end of your communication you must remind your audience of each of your three sub-topics and highlight a key piece of evidence for each. When you do this effectively, your listeners will have no doubt that you know what you're talking about.

THE DIAMOND
STEP 5 - SUMMARIZE YOUR SUB-TOPICS

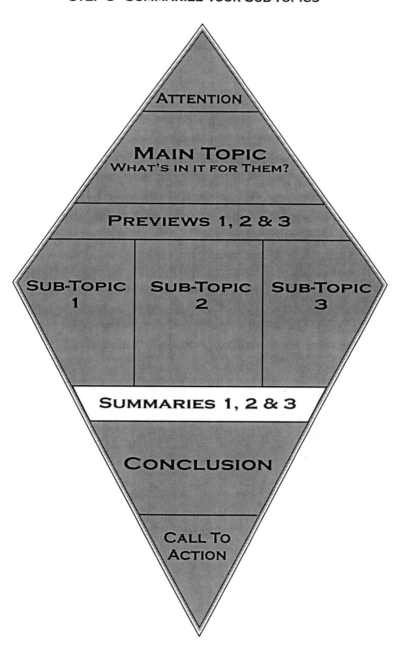

Chapter Sixteen

AND IN CONCLUSION
Make Your Point!

While every part of THE DIAMOND is important, your conclusion is critical. The conclusion serves as your key takeaway. Said another way, if there was one thing your listener should remember, it's your conclusion. A conclusion is a tight, well-focused distillation of everything you've talked about, so be sure to keep it brief. A conclusion that goes on for five minutes doesn't sound like much of a conclusion does it? Try to keep it to one sentence. Here are three examples of conclusions:

"The employee who is most likely to succeed at this company is the one who gets the highest customer satisfaction ratings."

"Des Moines has seen the lowest rate of unemployment in nearly three decades due to the influx of technology companies."

"The reason the elephants aren't eating is because the monkeys are mocking them."

THE DIAMOND
STEP 6 - MAKE YOUR CONCLUSIVE POINT

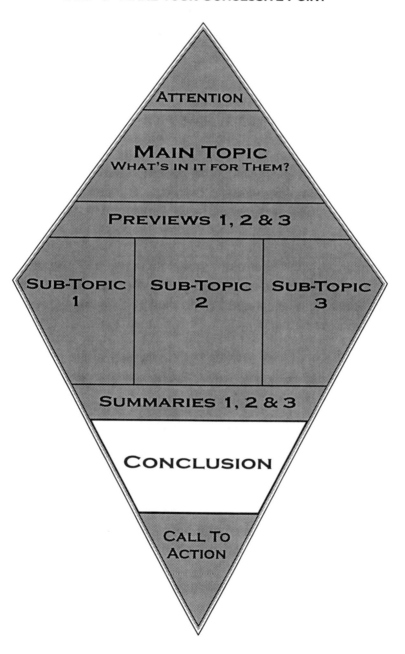

CHAPTER SEVENTEEN

ACTION JACKSON

WHAT DO YOU WANT THEM TO DO?

The VP of Sales can tell her team, "We're spending too much on overhead." But unless she specifically states, "You have to cut back on your monthly expenses by 20%," nothing may change.

A store manager may say, "Our customer satisfaction numbers are slipping." But unless he says, "I want you to look every customer right in the eye, smile at them and say 'Have a great day!'" nothing may change.

A father can say, "Your room looks like a pig sty." But unless he says, "Pick up your underwear and make your bed in the next five minutes" nothing may change. (Even then nothing may change, but at least dad is being clear!)

The final step in THE DIAMOND is the action (or appeal) step. This is where the speaker tells the listener exactly what she would like him to do.

A very common pitfall with spoken communication is that the speaker leaves the listener hanging. In other words, the speaker doesn't specify what they would like to see happen next. Rather, they stop at the conclusion stage and assume that the listener will know what to do. Unless you state clearly what you want to occur next, you can almost assume that nothing will happen, or the wrong thing will happen. As one of our client's once told us: "If at the end of your presentation you don't owe somebody something or somebody doesn't owe you something, then what was the point of your presentation?"

THE DIAMOND
STEP 7 - TELL THEM WHAT YOU WANT TO HAPPEN

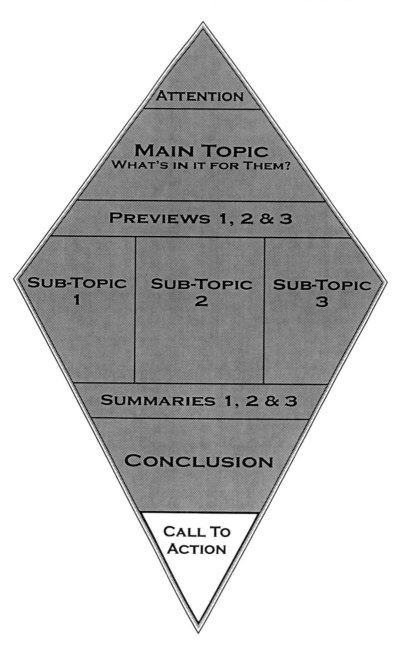

We suggest you try the "So what?" test. It's essential that you put yourself in your listener's shoes and ask: "So what does the speaker want me to do?" If you do this you will become much more conscious of what you'd like your listener to do and therefore you'll state it clearly. Don't assume that what's obvious to you will be obvious to them.

CHAPTER EIGHTEEN

THE DIAMOND SPARKLES

A SAMPLE PRESENTATION

THE DIAMOND model works for both you *and* your listener. You'll always know where you are in your presentation…and so will your listener. Your most difficult task is selecting the three ideas or sub-topics which embrace everything you want to say and that are easy to grasp and be remembered by those to whom you are speaking.

Here's a sample presentation of how one of our clients used THE DIAMOND format; his subject was about his hobby, wine collecting.

He opened with a lighthearted story (an attention getter) about how he recently forgot his 20th wedding anniversary until the day before. So at the last minute he hired a good caterer, broke out his best whites and reds and he and his wife had "the most romantic candlelit dinner we've had in twenty years."

He then stated his main topic: "Today I want to talk about wine collecting, a hobby of mine for the past 20 years." Next he previewed his three sub-topics. First, where the great wines are coming from and how to get good value when you buy. Second, how to make sure you get good selection and quality in wines when you dine out. And third, the secrets of successfully storing wines so you don't wind up with a bottle of vinegar.

His three sub-topics in the talk were well scoped out and he provided evidence for his assertions. For his first sub-topic he gave a

THE DIAMOND
WILL MAKE YOUR PRESENTATION SPARKLE

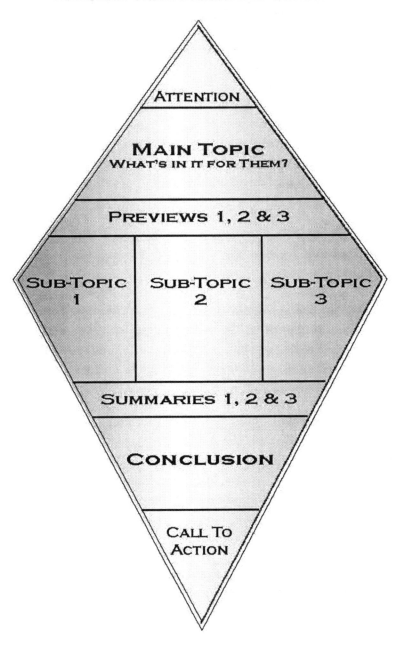

ATTENTION

MAIN TOPIC
WHAT'S IN IT FOR THEM?

PREVIEWS 1, 2 & 3

SUB-TOPIC 1

SUB-TOPIC 2

SUB-TOPIC 3

SUMMARIES 1, 2 & 3

CONCLUSION

CALL TO ACTION

tour of the globe including vineyards, wineries and best values. For number two, he gave a great lesson on wine lists and how to interview a maitre d' on the phone when making restaurant reservations. And for sub-topic three, he gave a primer on wine cellars and a few tips on storing wines in your own home. (Can you see that each one of these points has a *benefit*, or WIIFM, for the listener?)

Now to the summaries. For the first, he summed up the best way to get value when buying wines. To reinforce number two, he gave us a list of some restaurants close by with good wine lists. And for three, we got a few more ideas on storing wines. Reinforcement, reinforcement, reinforcement.

In his conclusion (which is often a reinforcement of the main topic) he stated that collecting wines is a great hobby where you can travel, drink and make money if you trade wines.

His appeal/action step? He told his listeners to subscribe to *The Wine Spectator* and visit his favorite retailer.

So the next time you have to run a meeting, speak on a conference call or give a new business pitch...try THE DIAMOND. It works.

Chapter Nineteen

THE 15-SECOND PROMO
THE ESSENCE OF YOUR MESSAGE

Ever notice that when you're sitting on the couch watching TV, about ten minutes before the news comes on the network tries to grab you with a real quick promo? It happens all the time. The networks know how to package the half-hour news into a very short 15-second "grabber" that pulls you in. They do the same thing for their sitcoms, talk shows, dramas and reality shows. And they're really good at it.

It's the same way in advertising. Advertising, when done well, is the ultimate communication medium. Advertisers have to persuade you *and* they don't have much time with which to do it. What a challenge!

Here's how the process works: After the client hires the advertising agency, the agency spends months researching the product and consumer. They do quantitative and qualitative studies up the ying-yang. (That can't be comfortable.) Then, after reams of research are generated, the agency puts together a one-page creative strategy brief derived from all that data. The creative strategy brief highlights who's the target audience and what the main message should be. Next, sample ads are created and tested until the final T.V. spot or print ad is chosen.

Months of research, a ton of data and the agency's creative team has to boil it down to a compelling 15 or 30-second commercial!

In order to make your point, you, too, need to be able to do what great advertising people do: boil your message down to its essence.

By being able to do this, you will be crystal-clear about what you're trying to convey.

When we coach our clients, we do an acid test with them and challenge them to articulate their *entire message* in less than 15 seconds, almost as if it were a TV spot. We want them to be able to *succinctly* state two things in that very short period of time: First, what's their main point? And second, why should their listener care? If our clients can give an effective 15-second promo, then we know they have a well-focused message.

One time we were hired by a client who was preparing to give a presentation to a thousand people from all over the world. When we met with him, his presentation was just about finished and he had about 35 PowerPoint slides chock-full of information. We asked him to take us through his material. After about five minutes into it (with our heads about to implode from all the data he dumped on us) we stopped him and asked: "What's the *one thing* you want your audience to remember when you're finished?" Do you know what he said? He said: "I'm not really sure." The irony, of course, is that he was all set to give his presentation, yet he couldn't tell us what his point was.

There's an old story about David Mamet, the famous Broadway producer who, whenever asked by playwrights to consider producing their works, would hand them his business card and ask them to write their idea on the back of his card. Why? Well Mamet felt that if a playwright could clearly state what the concept was in very few words, then the playwright had a clear vision and Mamet would be willing to talk to him about producing it.

Here's the 15-second promo for this book: **Make Your Point! is a book that teaches you how to speak clearly and concisely anyplace anytime. If you do what the authors tell you, this book will help you be more persuasive, gain more respect, and move up in your organization faster.**

Chapter Twenty

DON'T DO A DATA DUMP

Ease up on facts and figures.

Ah, the dreaded data dump. We've all been victims of this all-too-common type of communication. And perhaps a few of us have even been perpetrators. (You know who you are.) A data dump happens when a speaker does a boatload of research and for some reason feels compelled to share *all* of it with his listeners. Most often it's in the form of dastardly PowerPoint slides loaded with numbers, or, in white collar parlance, "metrics." But data dumps can even happen in one-on-one conversations. The problem with the information overload approach is that it's boring, it's confusing, it's unwanted and it's often useless. So why do people do it?

For starters, dumping a bunch of numbers on your listeners somehow feels safer to the speaker than actually having to look people in the eye and connect with them. There's a comfort level when we hide behind lots of numbers. Secondly, it's a smokescreen; if we just show lots of data, then maybe our listener won't notice we're not making a point. And lastly, it makes the speaker look smarter, because he mistakenly thinks that data = information = smart.

Here's what one of your authors experienced firsthand during a "data dump" a number of years ago...

"There we were, in a darkened, stuffy conference room. The presenter was well into the second hour of a deadly three-hour research overview. It felt to many of us that boredom would bring about our untimely deaths. As the researcher was droning on, the person sitting next to me suddenly gave out a loud yelp and jumped back from the conference table. The outburst startled everyone, most of whom were asleep at the time, and disrupted the meeting for a few moments. Once everything got back to order, the presenter drudged on.

After the meeting, I caught up with the screamer and asked him what caused him to suddenly cry out in the meeting. He confided in me that he had become so bored with the presentation that he had turned his attention to the whirling fan inside the overhead projector. So captivated was he by the strobing propeller, that he took out his pencil and started playing "chicken" with it. As he was poking inside the projector, the fan unexpectedly caught his pencil and snapped it out of his hand. This so surprised him that he screamed."

So what's our point? Well, if the fan on the projector is more interesting than your presentation, then you need to rethink your presentation. Ease up on the numbers and *connect* with your listeners. Don't just give them data; tell them what all the data *means* to them and their business. Add value.

SECTION
THREE

DELIVERY

MAKE YOUR POINT!

Chapter Twenty One

THE LAW OF RECIPROCITY
Life's a boomerang!

Everyone's familiar with the law of gravity. It's all around us, it's pretty darn powerful, it's invisible, and it affects everything we do. Yet we don't think about it too much do we? It's just there. Well there's another law that, in a sense, is the human equivalent of the law of gravity. It, too, is all around us, is very potent, has a profound influence on all of us and, like gravity it is invisible. It's called the Law of Reciprocity. And when you become more aware of the Law of Reciprocity, it can absolutely help you become more persuasive.

The Law of Reciprocity is quite simple. Essentially it says that people react to us the same way we act towards them. In other words, human emotions and behaviors are contagious. People automatically reflect back the way they are treated (or perceive they are treated). If Denise believes she's being respected, she, in turn, gives respect back. If she feels she's being dismissed, she'll become dismissive. Reciprocity has been bred into us over millions of years and is an instinctive human trait. Road rage is an example of the negative side of reciprocity. Exchanging gifts is the positive side.

So what does reciprocity have to do with helping you make your point? It's simple. Making your point has as much to do with *how* you say something as it does with *what* you say.

When you work in concert with The Law of Reciprocity, you realize that you can have an invisible, yet profound effect on how well you communicate with others. Non-verbal cues such as a smile, eye contact, standing upright and all those other seemingly superficial little things can have an amazing effect on how persuasive you are.

When you speak with energy, others will be more apt to listen. When you look at them, they'll look at you. When you add emphasis to words, you telegraph that you truly believe what you're saying. You have the power to set the tone for *any* conversation you have. Recently, one of your fine-feathered authors had to have a physical for insurance purposes. When the author called to set up the appointment with the doctor, the doctor sounded gruff and impersonal. There was no energy in the doctor's voice, no pleasant tone, no humor, no nothin'. When the author met the doctor in person, it was the same thing. The doctor hardly gave a greeting and generally seemed like a miserable slug. During the exam the author decided to strike up a conversation and asked the physician how he liked his job. The doctor responded: "The job's fine, except that I come across a lot of rude, nasty people." Of course he does! That's because *he's* the major cause of all that rude, nasty behavior.

Look around and you will see The Law of Reciprocity all over the place. Are you making it work for you or against you?

Chapter Twenty Two

A MATTER OF PERCEPTION

It's all about being capable and friendly.

You're at a party. A friend calls you over to introduce you to someone you've never met. You start a conversation with that person. How much time passes before you start sizing the person up and decide whether or not you like this person? Fifteen minutes? Ten? Five?

A study was done some years ago that found that during a job interview, 80% of the decision whether or not to hire someone was made within the *first three minutes* of the interview!

Does that surprise you? Probably not. When we share that statistic with our clients, the overwhelming majority of them agree with it. (Although one client of ours, the CEO of a small technology firm, disagreed. He told us he makes the majority of his decision within *two* minutes.) So that begs the question, how much substance do we get into in the first few minutes of a job interview or when we meet someone? Not much. That comes later on. In the first few minutes of an interview, we shake hands, get offered something to drink and engage in a little small talk. Yet the interviewer already has a good idea whether or not he'd hire us.

So what gives? How come humans base so much of their judgment about others on first impressions? Well, in order to understand this, one needs to understand a little bit about the physiology of the brain. (By the way, some of this comes from a terrific book written by Bert Decker called, *You've Got to be Believed to be Heard.*) The human brain is essentially made up of two parts: The outer brain and the inner brain. The outer brain, which is more commonly known as the cerebral cortex, is where all our conscious, higher level thinking takes place. This is where language skills, creativity and analysis go on. On the other hand, our inner brain (the limbic system and the brain stem) is where subconscious thought takes place. This is where our instinctive reactions and "gut" feelings about people come from. Our inner brain is *very influential* over how we perceive others. In a job interview, it's the inner brain of the interviewer that is trying to get a quick read on two fundamental questions: 1) Can this person do the job? 2) Do I like this person? (Will he fit in?) In short, they are sizing you up and trying to figure out: Are you *capable* and are you *friendly?*

An associate of ours, Pat Kirkland, of Skills for Success in Austin, Texas described it to us this way: "When you talk to others, not only are they listening to your words, but just as importantly…no, more importantly…they are quickly (and subconsciously) reading your non-verbal cues (body language, facial expressions, tone of voice) to determine: 1) Do you know what you're talking about and 2) Are you someone they can get along with?"

So it comes down to this: you become much more persuasive when others perceive you as both *capable* and *friendly*. In fact, when we work with customer service personnel, we videotape them and we coach them over and over on the behaviors that will help them *look and sound* both capable and friendly. If we can accomplish that, we know that they're going to be able to successfully manage virtually any customer interaction.

Are you the type of person that everyone likes being around because you're upbeat and fun, but perhaps you feel that you don't get as much respect as you deserve? If so, it could be because others may not *perceive* you as highly capable. You may need to work on behaviors such as: standing tall, giving a firm handshake, looking people right in the eye, not fidgeting and speaking more slowly.

Are you the type of person that people listen to because you command attention and you have an air of authority, but perhaps others don't feel comfortable around you? To them, you just seem to have an edge about you or you appear aloof. Maybe you're unknowingly alienating people because you're sending signals that you don't want to be around them. Start working on behaviors such as: smiling, making small talk, using people's names and talking with upbeat energy.

Perception is reality. In order to make our point, we need to be more aware of our behaviors so that we can better manage how others perceive us. Again, we want to be seen as both *capable* and *friendly*.

Read on, friends.

Chapter Twenty Three

THE ZONE SETS THE TONE

The power of positive energy

An associate of ours has two words above his computer in his office: "Energy Sells." It's his constant reminder that anytime he speaks on the phone he needs to raise his energy level. He knows from experience that if he communicates an *appropriate* level of enthusiasm, the listener/prospect will sense it and be more apt to want to meet him. This holds true not only in business, but in politics, sports, show biz and romance, too.

The chart in this chapter is absolutely key to helping you make your point. We call it *The Positive Energy Scale*. It's based on how much energy people *perceive* us as having. Our clients love this chart because it helps them quantify what they're already vaguely aware of. And for you it becomes a simple way to show you how others may perceive you.

In our estimation, over half (let's call it 60%) of the people we coach, are in the *Neutral* area. When they talk, they seem to have about average energy. Not bad, but not great either. A step below neutral is *Bad Day*. Based on our observations, about 15% of the population seems to be here. Even though these people may not actually be having a bad day, they *appear* to be and therefore bring down those around them. Common bad day behaviors include: not smiling, low volume, poor posture – you get the idea. In retail establishments across the US, you find the vast majority of customer service reps are either in neutral or in bad day mode. If they only kicked up their energy, what a difference they would see in their customers and their business!

At the bottom of the heap we find *Bad Life*. We all know a few of these miserable souls. If you ask a bad life person whether the proverbial glass is half full or half empty, they'd likely reply, "I didn't want any water anyway." The negative energy of a bad life person can suck the life out of a room. Thankfully, less than 5% seem to be languishing down here. The "Soup Nazi" from *Seinfeld* was a bad life type of person.

In the uppermost area we have *Over the Top*. These are the folks that we perceive as having *too much* energy. They speak too loudly, they sometimes invade other's personal space, they're overly enthusiastic and they sometimes don't appear genuine. Tony Robbins, Jim Carrey, Robin Williams and Howard Dean (remember his 2004 screamfest in Iowa?) are examples. The good news about this group is that at least they grab our attention and are often positive. We'd estimate that about 5% of the world lives here.

Finally, you've got the *In the Zone* crowd. Generally speaking, this is the magical place to be when you're communicating with others. The 15% of the population that are in the zone are the types of people that seem to light up a room when they walk in. They speak up, but not too loudly. They give good eye contact, but don't stare. They have a natural ease with people and a good sense of humor. They smile. When we coach out clients, we work to get them in the zone. Morning talk show hosts like Katie and Matt are in the zone people. So are George Clooney and Ellen DeGeneres.

For many years, there's been a doorman at The Adolphus Hotel in Dallas, Texas by the name of Philip Johnson. The moment you meet Philip you know he's in the zone. In fact, he's such a great communicator that his manager doesn't allow him to compete with his co-workers for the employee of the year award because he always wins it. What's Philip's secret? It all has to do with his behaviors. He has great posture, he looks people in the eye, he smiles, he shakes guests' hands, he speaks up and he jokes around. Philip gets it.

THE POSITIVE ENERGY SCALE
AIM TO BE "IN THE ZONE"

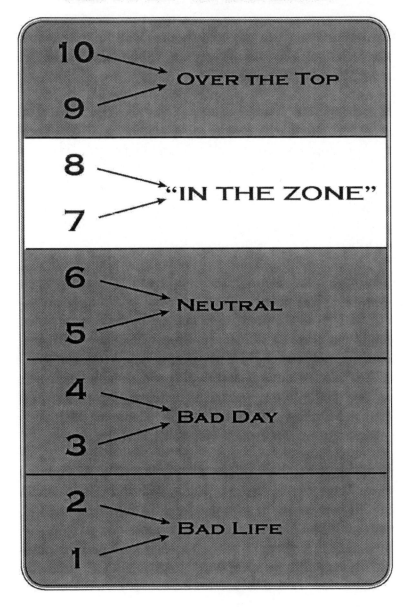

10
9 → OVER THE TOP

8
7 → "IN THE ZONE"

6
5 → NEUTRAL

4
3 → BAD DAY

2
1 → BAD LIFE

Sometimes our clients push back when we try to coach them to be in the zone. They say something like, "I feel like you're trying to make me into something I'm not. I'm a cello and you're trying to make me in to a piano." Our response to that is "You're a cello and we want you to stay a cello, but you're out of tune."

Being in the zone is not easy for many people, but when they go there, they immediately get a more positive response from others.

CHAPTER TWENTY FOUR

CONFIDENCE SELLS

OWN THE ROOM.

There is no substitute for confidence. Confidence, as we know, comes from within. When we feel an inner peace or inner strength, it shows on the outside. When we're confident, we smile, we look people in the eye and we stand tall. It's these external cues that our listeners see and then influences them to conclude that we must know what we're talking about because we sure *look* like we know what we're talking about. When you're confident, you're convincing.

But confidence doesn't always come from within. In fact there are plenty of people who really do know what they're talking about, but the way they say it sounds hesitant and unsure. And then their listener becomes skeptical and therefore much harder to persuade.

An interesting experiment we witnessed revealed some intriguing insight about how we perceive confidence. We once heard about a performance where a hypnotist asked a woman to come up on stage in front of an audience. (The woman had previously described herself to the hypnotist as extremely shy and very uncomfortable in front of crowds.) When she stood up before the audience, she truly was quaking in her boots. She gave every indication that she felt miserable up there...she stared downward, hunched her shoulders and didn't smile. The audience saw a frightened doe.

The hypnotist then went to the side of the stage and asked the painfully shy woman to join him. They stood off-stage for about 15 seconds and when they reappeared, the woman marched across the stage, stood tall in front of the audience, smiled and exuded confidence. The audience was amazed. What could the hypnotist possibly have done that transformed her?

When we pose this question to our clients, some suggest he hypnotized her, of course. Others say that he told her: "Believe in yourself!" or "You can do it!" Nope. It's much simpler than that. The hypnotist simply said, "I want you to stand up straight, walk to the center of the stage, look people right in the eye, and smile." He told her to execute the *specific behaviors* that instantly telegraph: "I'm confident and I know what I'm talking about." Inside, the poor woman may still have been miserable, but on the outside, she looked like a Nobel Prize winner.

"Act the way you want to feel and soon you will feel the way you act."
-Anonymous

Chapter Twenty Five

THE EYES HAVE IT

Eye contact connects.

It's been said that the eyes are the window to the soul. When we look directly into someone's eyes, we can connect instantly. It may be a good or a bad connection, but a connection none-the-less.

In order to master the spoken word, we need to master the unspoken word. When we focus on the eyes of our listener, we send and receive volumes of information. Eye contact helps us determine if our listener is interested, if they're in agreement, if they're confused, or if they have any questions. Likewise, we can communicate the same back to the other person. It also helps build credibility which leads to trust which leads to persuasion.

Is there a downside to eye contact? Sure. If you stare, your listener may feel as though you're trying to intimidate. But if you give a nod of acknowledgement and a smile, any sense of intimidation can easily be buffered.

We are often asked: "When speaking to a large group, should the speaker try to maintain one-on-one eye contact with individuals in the audience?" Our answer: Absolutely. Of course the speaker can't have one-on-one eye contact with everyone, but she should single out a variety of people and connect with them individually.

And by the way, please don't stare at an imaginary dot on the center of your listener's forehead (as some people have been taught to do). If you do, it's going to look like you're staring at an imaginary dot on the center of their forehead. Not good.

CHAPTER TWENTY SIX

I SEE WHAT YOU MEAN

BODY LANGUAGE SPEAKS VOLUMES.

In the early 1960's, UCLA Professor Albert Mehrabian conducted a research study to better understand human communication. Specifically, he wanted to figure out how much of the *meaning* of our messages comes from the words we use, how much comes from the sound of our voice, (such as our volume, pace, inflection, pitch) and how much comes from the way we look (which includes facial expressions, hand gestures, body language, clothing, and eye contact). While his results surprised many, for others it reinforced what they had long suspected.

Mehrabian's study revealed that in spoken communication, humans derive 7% of the *meaning* of the message from the words (the verbal), 38% from the sound of the voice (the vocal) and a whopping 55% from what we see (the visual)! (Perhaps this explains why supermodels make more money than poets.) While these findings are fascinating, one should use these figures as a guide and not as a direct conclusion about degrees of effectiveness to each and every communication situation. With that said, if you were to adjust the numbers and say that all three elements are equally important, that still means that two thirds of the *meaning* of one's message comes from non-verbal cues. (Incidentally, Mehrabian also discovered that when speaking on the phone, 82% of the meaning comes from the *sound* of the voice and 18% comes from the words.)

To better illustrate Mehrabian's study, in our workshops we will often look at a participant and exclaim: "Nice shirt!" We say it with upbeat energy and a smile and the person immediately beams. Moments later we say the same exact words to someone else, but this time we roll our eyes and deliver the line with a sarcastic tone:

"Nice shirt!" Immediately that person feels deflated or ticked-off. Same words, yet an entirely different meaning due to our visual and vocal cues.

Try this experiment. Say the following sentence out loud: "Dave didn't say Julie took the papers." (For your own sake, we suggest you do this when no one is around.) Now say that same sentence seven more times, but each time you say it, emphasize a different word in the sentence. You'll see that you'll end up with seven very different meanings for that one sentence. This might shed a little light on why we have so many misunderstandings with others and also why email is so often misinterpreted and can cause lots of problems.

So what does all this mean to you? Well, if you're like many people, you spend almost all of your time before you speak preparing the words you're going to say. That's fine. Words *are* important. However, do you spend enough time thinking about *how* you're going to say them?

CHAPTER TWENTY SEVEN

GESTICULATE ALREADY

GESTURE TO REINFORCE IDEAS.

OK, so you're sitting across the desk from an unenergized person who's delivering a series of dull, boring messages and you're wondering when the police will be there to outline his body with chalk. A real stiff. Has this person been embalmed already or is it just someone not using their non-verbal communications skills?

Delivering the spoken word, whether presenting across the desk or in front of a big group, should be an orchestration of every communication tool available to you: the brain, the voice and the body. And we mean the *whole* body...facial expressions, arm and hand gestures and the position of the torso. Social scientists tell us that audiences (anyone looking at and listening to you) will derive more meaning from your visual image than from your words.

Our work has proven that gesturing, the use of any and all body parts (within reason, of course) comes directly from enthusiasm and passion. They should come from your natural style and your willingness to let your body do some of the talking. Keep your arms loose and your hands in front of you lightly clasped so you can use them openly and freely when you want. Stand erect but not stiff. Be aware that every part of your face...eyebrows, cheeks, mouth and eyes can gesture. Your body language should *reinforce* your words. When you say something like: "the entire portfolio," then use open arms to illustrate something all-encompassing. When you say: "we have tight margins," then use your hand gestures to show something that's small. Practice by standing in front of a full-length mirror and observe your gestures. It'll teach you a lot.

And be careful not to penalize yourself by keeping your hands in your pockets, or crossed in front of you or twiddling a pencil.

Good communication will come from alertness and the ability to let your face and your body language help sell your points.

Chapter Twenty Eight

DRONES GET GROANS

Vary your voice.

Are you aware of those "white noise" machines? You know, the ones that muffle office or home ambient noise. When you deliver your message without modulating the range or varying the volume of your voice, you become a white noise machine; nothing more than a pulsating piece of equipment that no one really listens to. You become background noise.

Anti-droning can be accomplished if you concentrate on two behaviors...using inflection to add meaning to your words and using the changing volume and pacing to dramatize points.

First, inflection. Most adjectives and nouns have a meaning all their own and we need to pronounce them as such. A few examples: The word "huge" means really, really big and needs to be said that way. "Exciting" is an emotional word that suggests energetic delight. Deliver it that way. And a billion of anything is a lot. Make it sound like a lot. Inflection adds meaning. Try saying, "There is a *huge* audience of over a *billion* people out there, and boy is that *exciting.*"

Secondly, volume and pacing. Imagine an EKG monitor that shows peaks and valleys. That's the type of readout you should shoot for when you talk. The peaks in the chart are where your voice is faster paced and the loudest. The valleys are where you slow down, lower your volume and deliver more deliberately. Again, your content will have more meaning and impact when you *vary* how you deliver it. If you flatline, so will your listener.

CHAPTER TWENTY NINE

PUMP UP THE VOLUME

PROJECT YOUR VOICE.

In an earlier chapter, we talked about the importance of being *in the zone*. While there are many behaviors that can help us get in the zone, by simply raising the volume of your voice you can get there quicker and more easily.

In one-on-one communication, speaking louder than normal isn't necessary and would be annoying. There is an intimacy in one-on-one discourse that doesn't necessitate a strong voice. But when you're conversing with two or more people, your volume may need to come up a notch in order to help command attention. In a conference room with 10 to 15 listeners, kick it up even higher. And when you're in front of a large audience, take it up more.

We have to tell a lot of our clients to speak louder, whether they're speaking in front of a group, on a conference call or leaving a voicemail. Rarely do we need to tell someone to lower their volume. Ironically, in one of our sessions we had exact opposites: the mutterer and the screamer. The first could barely be heard over the sound of the air conditioner, the second threatened to cause chronic hearing problems if contained in the room with him for more than a day. Neither of them had their volume set at the right level.

Because there's a gap between how loud we *think* we're speaking and how loud we actually *are* speaking, many people find it hard to believe they need to raise their voice. We suggest you ask a trusted colleague what they think about your volume. Also, test out your volume in the room where you'll be speaking, keeping in mind that when a room is full, you'll need to speak even louder.

CHAPTER THIRTY

SILENCE IS GOLDEN

PACE YOURSELF AND ADD PAUSES.

Do you, as do so many others, believe that "timing is everything?" Well when you communicate, timing truly *is* everything.

When you read an article or a book, you come across many forms of punctuation: commas, periods, dashes, colons and semi-colons. In oral communication you don't have punctuation…no commas to signal a series of things or periods to signal the end of a sentence. All you have are pauses. The length of the pause is determined by the kind of punctuation you would see in written communication. A slight pause for commas, a little longer for periods and colons, and longer still for paragraphs. And really good, long, pauses when the topic changes (like it does between segments within THE DIAMOND model).

Let's say you're talking to someone and you're reciting a series of three things like "yesterday, today, and tomorrow." In offering this orally, it should be "yesterday (slight pause) today (slight pause) and tomorrow (slight pause)." Don't rush it. Take your time to make it work.

While pauses that signify commas, periods, and dashes may be one second or less, longer pauses of two to four seconds should be used to signify a change of topic. Here's an analogy. When you read a book, you'll notice that when a chapter ends, there is a partial blank page or sometimes a full blank page. This gives the reader time to regroup and refocus before moving on to a new idea. Your long pauses do the same thing for your listener when you change topics. And pauses allow you to catch your breath. Pauses are not "dead-air." They are your way to *punctuate* your talk.

Incidentally, John Menzer, who is CEO of Wal-Mart International, told us he learned the importance and acceptance of pauses while in Japan. His speech was fed to the audience by an interpreter. By necessity he was forced to speak one sentence at a time and then wait for the interpretation sentence-by-sentence. It was then that he found that pauses can be very effective.

Great speakers can mesmerize us and have us hang on every word as they manipulate us with their pauses and timing. As a colleague of ours once said: "I don't teach public speaking. I teach public pausing. Anybody can speak in public, but it's really hard to pause in public." You'll see some of the best presenters sip water while they're speaking. Not only is this to lubricate their vocal chords, but it forces them to pause.

CHAPTER THIRTY ONE

CAUTION: WORD OVERLOAD

TOO MUCH INFORMATION!

We considered titling this book *An Instructive Guide that will Show You a Variety of Tools and Techniques You Can Use to Develop and Deliver a Message that Communicates the Essence of Your Thought Process in a Cohesive, Cogent and Convincing Manner.* Kind of catchy isn't it? But after much soul-searching we decided to go with *Make Your Point!*

There are two reasons why people use more words when they could use fewer: First, they probably aren't clear in their own head what they're trying to say. Their mouth leads and their brain follows. Good communicators, however, know what they want to say *before* they say it and can get right down to it. Do you know what you're trying to say before you speak?

Second, assuming they do know what they want to say, but they still use too many words, then they just aren't disciplined. Our friends in advertising know about discipline. When the cost of a 30-second ad on a successful primetime show costs almost a half-million smackers, words are at a premium. Advertising people spend months researching their client's product or service and then they boil all that knowledge down to a very brief TV commercial or print ad. Example: *Volvo is the safest car on the road today.* Got it.

When the great orator William Jennings Bryan accepted the Democratic nomination for President in 1896, the average length of a sentence in his speech was 104 words. Today, the average length of a sentence in a political speech is less than 20 words. We're simply in an age of directness and making our point more quickly.

Next time you have to make a point, imagine you had to say it in a 15-second ad. This will force you to get right down to it.

Words are like money. Why spend more when you can spend less? Talk as if you're on a budget.

Chapter Thirty Two

BUZZWORDS, JARGON, DOUBLESPEAK

Avoid gobbledygook.

If you leverage robust venues, practice 24/7, think outside the box and optimize results-driven values, you'll find a synergistic win-win client-focused mind-set for speaking effectively. Boy, isn't that clear and concise?

Why do people fall into the jargon trap? It's probably for peer acceptance or to show that they're as smart as the next person. But are you that smart if half your audience doesn't understand what you're saying?

If you're the kind of person who is drowning in bureaucratic jargon, please resist it. A Medicare official once talked about "the ultimate negative healthcare patient outcome." Only Medicare insiders knew he was talking about death. And speaking of death, some health insurance companies define death as "involuntary disenrollment." Don't you just love it? It doesn't sound so bad that way, does it? Too bad most people don't know what the heck "involuntary disenrollment" means. Buzzwords, jargon and doublespeak will be the *death* of our language.

Not so long ago, a consulting firm came out with a software program called *Bullfighter* that edits out jargon. *The New York Times*, in announcing it, stated: "The people blamed for incentivizing companies to repurpose, build mindshare and utilize change agents have taken aim at their own lingo."

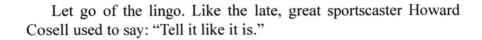

Let go of the lingo. Like the late, great sportscaster Howard Cosell used to say: "Tell it like it is."

CHAPTER THIRTY THREE

I THINK, MAYBE, PROBABLY

GET RID OF QUALIFIERS.

We recently worked with the head of research for a major corporation. In presenting the findings of three studies, he prefaced his results for the first with "I think," the second with "maybe," and the third with "probably." Unfortunately for him, he sounded more like a timid game show contestant than the head of research for a big company.

Why do so many people precede declarative statements with qualifiers like "I think," "maybe," and "probably?" These words dilute your role and your credibility.

Don't say: "I think we need this program." Say: "We need this program." Don't say: "Maybe this program will resolve the issue." Say: "I'm confident this program will resolve the issue." Don't say: "People will probably react to this issue favorably." Say: "Experience shows that similar programs have impressed people."

Often, the term "I think" pops into our conversations involuntarily. It's almost like an "uhm" or an "ahh." It's a bad affectation. Tape yourself and listen for the "I thinks," "probablys" and "maybes."

Declarative statements shouldn't be diluted by qualifiers unless you *intentionally* want to qualify them.

CHAPTER THIRTY FOUR

ADD SIZZLE

ANALOGIES, SURPRISING STATISTICS AND HUMOR

A few years ago, one of our clients was running a meeting and he talked about how to plan effectively. He said that when you plan, if you don't factor in what has happened in the past, then "it's like planting cut flowers and expecting them to grow." That's sizzle.

In the beginning of this book we talked about using an attention getter to hook your listener. Along the same lines, we find that the best communicators are the ones who add attention getters to *keep* their listeners engaged. Here are samples of a few different devices you should try.

Analogies are the communicator's ace in the hole. When used well, analogies can help clarify complex ideas, bring life to boring subjects and make concepts stick. A fifth-grader by the name of Collin had to give a presentation to his classmates on the pancreas. He had discovered that the pancreas performed two primary functions: It secretes enzymes to digest food and it secretes insulin to regulate blood sugar. Collin told his classmates that the pancreas was a lot like a football coach; it knows when to send in the offense (enzymes) and when to send in the defense (insulin). That's communication.

Surprising statistics are great. Don't just recite boring numbers. Find numbers that get your listener to say: "You're kidding me, I didn't know that!" An article in the August 17, 1998 issue of *The New Yorker* revealed this surprising statistic: "The typical mutual fund investor expects annual returns from the stock market of thirty-four percent over the next ten years which implies that the Dow will be at 136,500 in 2008." That's a grabber.

Humor. No, we're not suggesting you start your next conversation with your CEO by saying, "So a nun and a rabbi walk into a bar." But we are saying that you should find ways to add a little levity when you're speaking to others. People who have a good sense of humor and can laugh at themselves are more interesting to listen to and are more persuasive. Lighten up. One client kicked off a conference by saying: "Here are the Top Ten Reasons we decided to hold this year's meeting in New Mexico during the summer..."

Send us an email (Kevin@kevincarroll.com) and we'll be happy to send you a list of ***22 Ways to Add Sizzle.***

Chapter Thirty Five

SO WHAT'S YOUR STORY?

Stories are hooks.

A woman in one of our classes told this story: "When I was in college, I was awfully tired one particular morning because I had been up very late studying. I was thinking about skipping my morning class to catch up on my sleep, but being the conscientious student that I was, I decided to go anyway. I got to my class early and sat up front figuring that would help keep me awake, but unfortunately I dozed off. When I awoke, I received a standing ovation from the class. And if that wasn't bad enough, I then realized that I had slept through my entire class and the people applauding for me were from the following class!" She then made this point: "If you replenish your resources early on, you won't run short when you need them later."

There are so many ways to make your message come alive and to help make it stick with your listener. One of the most compelling things you can do is to tell a personal story that helps you make your point. Stories grab attention. Stories inspire. Stories comfort the soul. Some Fortune 500 companies even offer workshops to their employees on how to use personal stories to be more persuasive. Witness the success of the *Chicken Soup* book series...stories, stories, stories.

Why are stories so important? It could be that humans have been telling them for eons and they're part of our nature. Or it could be because others can relate to us better through our stories. Whatever the reason, the best communicators use personal stories and experiences to make their content come alive.

Using a personal story to help make your point is a simple one-two process. First, share a personal experience that you know gets a reaction from people. For example, it could be about the time you accidentally backed your father's car into a lake. Second, make *one* crystal-clear point from that experience and *bridge* that point to your listener. Based on the lake story, the point could be: "If we take the time to plan ahead, we won't have any disastrous results."

Tell a story, make one point and bridge it to your listener. They'll remember the story, they'll remember your point and they'll remember you.

Chapter Thirty Six

PLEASE LEAVE A MESSAGE

Making voicemail work for you

A few days before one of our coaching sessions, we listened to a voice mail from one of our students. Here it is: "Thought I'd check in on our session for next week. Have some new thoughts, but, you know, we may or may not want to discuss them. I don't know if I'll be around before the session. What do you think?"

How many rambling, discombobulated voicemails do you get? You know, the all too long streams of consciousness that start no place and go nowhere. The ones that get you muttering: "What's his point? What does she want me to do?"

Too many people fail to construct and plan their voicemail messages in advance. They simply leave a message asking for a call back. Well that's okay sometimes, but other times the person needs you to leave specific information on their voicemail to solve their problem.

A number of our clients keep a copy of THE DIAMOND model near their phone so that they can streamline the voicemail messages they leave.

Here's a suggested way to deliver a tight voicemail message. Let's say you've just completed a major marketing survey. Your voicemail to the VP of Sales could sound something like this: "Jim, we've just finished the marketing survey you sponsored. There are three things you should know: First, I believe you will like the results; second, we need another two days to put the final report together, and, finally, I'm confident that the survey will significantly guide our product launch next month." And, then you add your action step:

"Please call me at your earliest convenience so we can discuss it in more detail."

Well constructed, clear, concise voicemails will save time and make your communications more effective. Speaking of THE DIAMOND, when you're about to have a phone conversation with someone and you have a bunch of issues to cover, use THE DIAMOND to help manage your call. A client of ours at Merrill Lynch told us that she used THE DIAMOND to run a conference call and immediately after she got off the phone one of the people on the call emailed her and told her that was the best conference call they had ever been on.

Chapter Thirty Seven

EMAIL THIS!

Making email work for you, too

Although this is a book on *speaking* clearly and concisely, we couldn't resist throwing in a chapter on email. On one level, email is a wonderful communication medium. It's quicker than a fax or a letter (remember letters?), it's not as interruptive as the telephone and, for the introverted types, it's a nifty way to avoid having any face-to-face contact. And it's free, too.

Now for the bad news...

Email can be a demon. You can't read the body language of the person who has sent it. You can't interpret voice inflection. And you can't ask for immediate clarification if you're confused. As wonderful as email is, it has baggage.

So how can you make email work for you? To answer that, we'll focus on two things: 1) Content and 2) Tone.

When it comes to content, heed the same principles we've outlined in this book: First, know your audience. (Who will it be sent to and who might it be *forwarded* to?) Second, know your objective. (Have you clearly stated what your purpose is?) And third, whenever appropriate, use THE DIAMOND format to structure your content and make it easier for the reader to digest your ideas. (Use fewer words, stick with threes and have an action plan.)

Tonality in email is tricky. Proofread your email as if *you* were the recipient. Does that little quip come off as intended or will it be misinterpreted as bitter or sarcastic? Do your words reflect exactly what you mean? Take the word "right," for example. By itself it could mean "I agree with you" or it could mean "I *don't* agree with you." Also, have you tried to inject a warm, friendly tone so that your reader will be more receptive? (Opening with "Hi Harry" rather than just "Harry" sets a more positive tenor.)

We'll there's lots more that could be said about email, but let us end by suggesting that you keep a list of the things that bother you about the emails you receive and then *avoid* doing those things when you write your emails.

CHAPTER THIRTY EIGHT

WHAT'S THE POINT OF POWERPOINT?

EFFECTIVE USE OF VISUALS

A recent Dilbert cartoon showed a PowerPoint moment: A person in the audience asks the speaker, "Did you intend the presentation to be incomprehensible, or do you have some sort of rare PowerPoint disability?"

Microsoft PowerPoint, and other presentation software like it, can be a wonderful tool to enhance the spoken word. When used well, it adds visual interest, reinforces words and provides a picture when only a picture will do. But if misused, as it often is, it becomes the black plague of the conference room...a dog's breakfast of gimmicks, gizmos and glitches. We're talking about bombs bursting in air, sliding and revolving lines of type, pulsating messages looking like a bad Times Square marquee and a barrage of microscopic data points appearing in a mind-numbing "build" or "reveal."

The problem is that in a fanciful, visually active presentation, most audiences will become dazzled by the graphics, but not the message. Don't let overstuffed graphics get in the way.

And while we're on the use of visuals, consider the two words in the term "visual aids." Yes, something visual that *aids* not distracts from or takes the place of the content of your presentation.

We have seen every violation of the basic rules of visual design including two-hundred data points per slide, jam-packed twenty-word sentences, graphics where graphics don't belong and tiny type. If we know the client well enough, we might wryly suggest: "Why don't you just put your slides up and say absolutely nothing." "Oh, but why would I do that?" they ask. Our answer is simple. "You wouldn't!" People can't read a data-intense slide *and* listen to you at the same time. So ease up on the data so they can listen to you. *You are the presentation, not your slides.*

Here's a suggestion. The next time you have to give a PowerPoint presentation, have two sets of slides. One is the presentation set which includes minimal data thus allowing you, the presenter, to flesh out the details when you speak. The other set can have more info on it and can be used as the handout version to be given *after* the presentation or if someone couldn't make it to your presentation.

As a rule of thumb, if you're using PowerPoint, 90% of the audience's attention should be on you and 10% on the slide. Not the other way around. Again, graphics should be visual aids not visual distractions. Learn how to make PowerPoint work for you.

And by the way, if your font size is smaller than 30 point, you're pushing it. Bigger is better.

SECTION
FOUR

HANDLING Q & A

CHAPTER THIRTY NINE

I'VE GOT A QUESTION

BE PREPARED; ANTICIPATE QUESTIONS.

Why would anyone present anything without anticipating the possible questions they might be asked? Sure, a good presentation should answer questions before they're asked (anecdotes, examples and statistics should be in place as evidence for assertions) but there will always be unanswered questions...and you should do your best to know what they are.

A recent *New York Times* op-ed piece on presidential press conferences stated that staff members can anticipate up to 95% of questions that will be asked. You, too, can anticipate questions by putting yourself in your listener's seat and looking at it from their perspective. For example, if you say: "We must initiate this program." The listener would likely ask: "Why?" If you say: "Our company is dominant in this marketplace." The listener would say: "Show me." If you say: "We need $200,000 to run the program." The listener would ask: "Why that amount?"

Time spent listing potential questions and forming answers will pay rich dividends. Anticipate 10 to 20 questions you're likely to be asked and anticipate 10 to 20 questions you hope you're never asked.

And if worse comes to worst, it is okay to say: "I don't have that information, but I'll get back to you with it."

Chapter Forty

GO ON OFFENSE

No need to be defensive.

An executive recently told us that in stressed, uncomfortable Q&A sessions, he feels like a hockey goalie. "The puck just keeps coming at me. All I can do is to try to keep the puck out of the net." A great image, but not a space *you* want to occupy. You want to get the puck up the ice and score goals.

We're not suggesting you become a control freak. You shouldn't do anything that cuts off participation and democracy. In fact, you should do everything to encourage dialogue and conversation. Control in Q&A sessions results from establishing yourself through your confident style and temperament.

Get your back away from the wall. Move forward. Connect with the audience through forward body language and effective eye contact. Create energy and enthusiasm in your voice which will establish a commanding presence.

Answers that are complete establish control. And answers that are delivered with conviction and provide support (evidence) for assertions present you as the expert. However, answers that leave doubt or automatically raise other questions diminish control which causes uneasiness in audiences.

Finally, we all have seen contentious, heated Q&A sessions. The trick here is patience. Lower the heat of the session by being composed and measured in your delivery. Most often, your composure, along with the audience's peer pressure, will wilt the aggressor and the session will go back to normal.

To sum it up, forget about playing defense in Q&A sessions. A comfortable, confident offense is king.

CHAPTER FORTY ONE

LISTEN UP

LISTENING SKILLS ARE KEY TO Q & A.

Have you ever sat in a meeting and heard someone say something like: "Our plants are located in New York, Florida and California." And then some knucklehead asks: "Are your plants all in one region or spread throughout the country?"

In order to communicate effectively, we need to *listen* well.

Here are some tips to help you improve your listening skills that, in turn, will help you become better at answering questions.

Read the other person's body language and facial expressions. Are they giving you non-verbal cues that say, "I don't know what the heck you're talking about? Or, "This is the dumbest idea I've ever heard." If so, stop talking and ask them what they're thinking. If you see things like a squint, furrowed brow or frown, then stop. Don't just keep plowing through.

Pay attention. When the other person asks you a question, really pay attention. Don't let your thoughts wander or anticipate what *you think* they're going to say. As they say in improvisational theater, *be in the moment* and commit to understanding what they're asking.

Ask for clarification. If you don't understand what they're asking, then don't try to answer the question. Either ask them to repeat their question, or paraphrase their question back to them to see if that's what they're asking.

Understand the question behind the question. People will often ask one question, when in fact they have an underlying question that's the one they really want to have answered. For example, someone asks you: "Are you free next Saturday?" They may be thinking anything from, *I hope you can join me for the seventh game of the World Series* to *I hope you can help me caulk my windows.* So, if on the surface you're not quite sure why they're asking a particular question, dig a little more so you understand what their underlying question is.

CHAPTER FORTY TWO

BRIDGE THE GAP
REPACKAGE QUESTIONS.

In the old Road Runner cartoons, the bird often came to the edge of a cliff, put on the brakes and somehow figured out a way to propel himself over the gap. It's kind of like that when difficult questions are posed to us in a probing, pressing fashion. It makes us want to get to safer ground…to bridge the gap. How can I field the question, yet get over to the other side and make my point?

The technique, as you may have guessed, is called "bridging"… building a verbal bridge…a transitional phrase…to that safer, more affirmative ground. You might face a question with a nasty preface, a question intended to trap you, or a question showing how what you're proposing has failed in the past. At that instant, you need time to come at the answer from a different direction and to reposition yourself.

One time, a questioner had suggested to one of our clients that our client's new business launch was "ill timed in these tough economic conditions and doomed to failure." Our client answered: "Let me put that into perspective (the bridge). In this economy, our customers have even *more* pressure to improve the bottom line and we can help them do just that." Well done. Another time, a client had a detailed, complex negative question to handle. The opening to the answer (the bridge) was: "That's a complicated question, let me put it into context for you…" and then he went on to the central message in the direction he chose himself.

There is no federal law that requires you to jump into an answer precipitously. Take your time and be contemplative. A friend of ours recently showed a natural inclination to "hang back" and form a good answer before he started talking. When asked if this came naturally, he said it was because of his mother. "There were hundreds of times when I was young and arrived home and my mother would say: 'Where have you been?' I needed time to think."

We're not suggesting that you avoid questions and give your questioner the runaround. However we are suggesting that there are times where you may need to *frame* your answer appropriately. When answering questions, make time for yourself and start from safe, solid territory.

Bridge over troubled waters.

CHAPTER FORTY THREE

BEGIN WITH THE CONCLUSION

HOW TO "HEADLINE" ANSWERS

So you ask a friend a question and as they're giving you a longwinded answer, you start muttering to yourself: "Get to the point! Get to the point!" What your friend needs to realize is that the most effective way to answer a question is to "headline" it. The way to do this is by stating the conclusion first (your headline) and then supporting the conclusion afterwards. Just like they do in the newspapers.

Let's say you're asked: "Does your program have any possible chance to succeed?" Bad starts for the answer are: "Well, let me tell you about the other programs that we had taken a look at." Or "In order to answer that question, I'd like to begin by telling you about how our program was developed." No, no, no! Conclusion first. "Our program will definitely succeed for three reasons. First..." and off you go.

A client of ours is CEO of a large manufacturing company. As an engineer, he used to have technical writers working for him. To support the concept of "headlining," he said he used to tell his writers to "*First* tell me what answer you got to and *then* tell me how you got there."

Chapter Forty Four

DON'T MAKE IT UP

Always aim to be correct and credible.

Did you ever try "the dog ate my homework" excuse and then your teacher found out that you didn't have a dog? Succinct answers are great, but answers that aren't true or leave out pertinent information are a no-no.

Not long ago, a spokesperson for a chemical company was questioned on a major network on health problems that might be caused by the gasoline additive his company manufactured. The question was: "Why are these people getting sick from the gasoline?" His answer: "I wasn't there, but I know that there was a price increase in the gasoline." The interviewer replied incredulously: "You mean people complained about severe headaches because the price of the gasoline went up?" Silence...a look of pain on the spokesperson's face. The interviewer persisted: "In your own mind, does that make any sense?" More pain, some uhhs and ahhs, lots of dead air...an embarrassing moment in front of twelve million viewers.

A real danger lurks in the use of statistics and other facts. If you think your company has 40% of the marketplace, be sure of the figure. If you think that there are 50,000 people in the program, confirm it before you use it.

Another danger is an assumption that there are easy answers to complicated questions. The great American writer H. L. Mencken once wrote: "There is always an easy solution to every human problem - neat, plausible, and wrong." Answers must paint a complete picture.

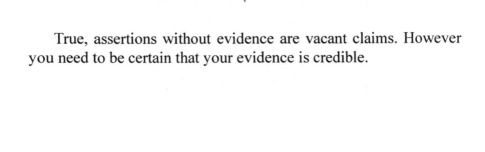

True, assertions without evidence are vacant claims. However you need to be certain that your evidence is credible.

CHAPTER FORTY FIVE

QUARRELSOME, CONTENTIOUS QUESTIONS

CONTROL YOUR AUDIENCE (IN A GOOD WAY).

Why do people ask questions in the first place? To get answers to things they're curious about, of course. Or to dig deeper into topics you've covered in your presentation. Those are positive reasons. Yet other people just want the exposure or want to look smart. Others may want to press you because they're in competition with you, or may just want to be contentious or quarrelsome because it's just how they are.

If you know your audience, you'll know how well prepared you must be for testy, confrontational, even rude questions. So what do you do when the going gets tough…when a barrage of aggressive questions are fired your way?

Patience is a virtue and composure a gift, but nowhere are they more effective than in difficult question sessions. If you get a little hot under the collar or cut the question off in the middle, no matter how long it is, you've lost the battle. Restrain yourself. Bite your tongue until it bleeds. And keep in mind that non-verbal communications are at a premium here. Establish strong eye contact with the questioner and keep a calm, composed facial expression.

Finally, audiences, in general, are usually "self-policing." A loud, out of control, self-aggrandizing questioner will usually be quieted by the rest of the audience through their groans, understated comments and their body language. If the questioner never gives up, and you've tried to answer their question, it's perfectly fine to suggest that you'd like to discuss it with them after the meeting

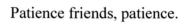

Patience friends, patience.

CHAPTER FORTY SIX

HONOR THY QUESTIONER
THE TECHNIQUE OF ANSWERING QUESTIONS

Maybe we've all been watching too many reality shows and crime dramas lately. You know, the type where some poor sap gets grilled during a cross examination. Sure, that happens occasionally, but for the most part, if you treat your questioner with respect, they'll do the same for you. With that said, here are eleven guidelines that should help you better manage your next question and answer session.

1. Create a list of the most likely questions you'll be asked and a list of the questions you hope you'll never be asked.

2. If possible, take questions *during* your presentation so that you can handle issues and objections as they come up. This also helps to build rapport between speaker and audience.

3. When taking questions at the end of your presentation, alert the audience a few minutes before you take the first question. This will allow them time to think up questions and not be caught off guard.

4. When you ask for questions, have a couple of your own questions ready to go so that if there is silence, you can say something like: "One question I'm often asked is..."

5. Be certain to listen to and *understand* the entire question. If necessary, paraphrase it to make sure you're clear on what's being asked. Also, listen for the question *behind* the question. (Why are they asking what they're asking?)

6. If you think the listener has asked an excellent, insightful question, then you can acknowledge that by saying "That's a good question." But don't overdo this, it sounds patronizing.

7. Answer the question! Concisely.

8. Support your answer with an example.

9. If you don't know the answer, say so. You can then ask if anyone in the room has the answer or you can promise to find the answer ASAP.

10. When dealing with hostile questioners, don't get defensive. Listen to them and validate their concerns. If they persist, tell them that in order to be fair to everyone else, you'd like to discuss their issues with them after the presentation.

11. End the question and answer period by recapping the key points from your presentation.

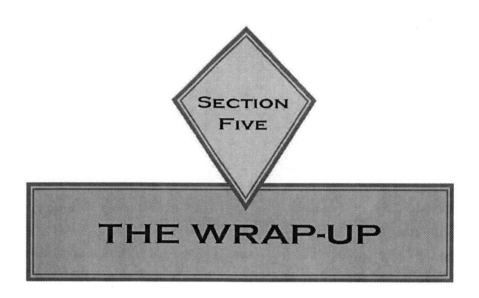

SECTION
FIVE

THE WRAP-UP

CHAPTER FORTY SEVEN

IT'S A TRUST THING

ARISTOTLE WAS A SMART GUY.

A driving force in getting your message across is being trustworthy. Our reputation is contingent upon whether or not we're credible, dependable, consistent and believable. Bend the truth or be seen as a flip-flopper and you've lost it.

Developing trusting relationships with those around you can take years. So what do you do when you're in front of people with whom you haven't had time to develop a trusting relationship? How do you establish trust? A good friend, Peter Morrissey, who runs a classy public relations company in Boston wrote a white paper on "Building a Base of Trust." He illustrated his point by citing "Aristotle's Approach" to rhetoric.

Aristotle's three intertwined principals are: *ETHOS, PATHOS* and *LOGOS* (well what do you know, once again a series of threes). *ETHOS* is all about moral character including reliability, integrity and reputation. You can't do much to change *ETHOS* when it's time to speak, so we'll assume that you wouldn't be where you are without an acceptable level of credibility and moral character. However, a calm, honest demeanor here will outwardly suggest trustworthiness.

On the flip side, you *can* do a lot to leverage *PATHOS* and *LOGOS* and make them work to your advantage. *PATHOS* is when you put conviction and passion to work. Passion plays to the listener's emotions giving you a chance to influence and persuade them. As Morrissey says, "Pathos can be used to arouse sympathy, provoke fear, or stimulate action." Almost every great speaker... Martin Luther King, Jack Kennedy, General George Patton, and

Vince Lombardi among many others…used passion to motivate and create action.

LOGOS means logic…does the *content* of what you're saying follow a sensible, easily understood path? This also means using facts in a reliable manner not misstating them or overstating them. The use of *evidence* backing up your assertions creates sustained interest and increased trustworthiness.

Bring Aristotle to the party and measure all of your communications against his *ETHOS, PATHOS,* and *LOGOS* approach. It works.

CHAPTER FORTY EIGHT

STUMBLING BLOCKS

THE TOP TEN COMMUNICATION ROADBLOCKS

As we head down the home stretch, it's a good idea to recap the top ten things that keep us from speaking clearly and concisely anyplace anytime.

1. We're not certain in our own minds what our point is before we start to speak. Therefore we tend to talk in circles and our listener gets confused.

2. We haven't used THE DIAMOND structure when we speak. Therefore our ideas run together and our listener finds it difficult to track with us.

3. We don't point out what the *benefits* are to the listener. Therefore the listener never really understands the *value* of what we have to say.

4. We talk too much and go off on tangents. Therefore the other person becomes bored and loses interest.

5. We use too much bizspeak or technical jargon. Therefore the listener gets lost trying to figure out what we're saying.

6. We give little or no eye contact. Therefore the other person isn't fully engaged in the conversation and we don't connect with them.

7. We speak with low energy or in a monotone. Therefore we don't grab the other person's attention and their thoughts start to wander.

8. We don't add much facial expression to what we're saying. Therefore we're not as interesting to listen to and our listener turns us off.

9. We speak too quickly. Therefore the other person can't follow us or might feel like they're being talked into something.

10. We haven't added attention getters, like analogies and stories, to what we're saying. Therefore our message becomes less memorable.

CHAPTER FORTY NINE

WHAT NEXT?

WHERE TO GO FROM HERE?

We're often asked: What can I do to get better at these skills? Well, just like the old joke: "How do I get to Carnegie Hall?" The same answer holds: "Practice, practice, practice."

You have to make *opportunities* for yourself. Take a leadership role in meetings. Articulate your point of view in front of others. Ask questions. Recap the meeting at the end. Volunteer to speak at the next conference. Provide value for others. Unless you *consciously* find ways to be seen and heard, you're going to get lost in the crowd.

By the way, there's an organization called Toastmasters International. It's kind of like a public speaking support group. You may want to contact them at www.Toastmasters.org or (949) 858-8255 to find a club near you. It's quite inexpensive and provides an informal atmosphere where you can practice your communication and speaking skills. While you won't receive professional coaching, you will get support and feedback from others. And when you're ready to move up to the big times, there's The National Speakers Association. NSA is made up of professional speakers and is a wonderful organization to help hone your platform skills and teach you how to market yourself as a speaker.

One more thought. Ask for input from those around you whom you respect. Find out if they think you communicate clearly. Ask them what they believe you do well and what they feel you could do better.

CHAPTER FIFTY

BE SEEN, BE HEARD

MARKETING YOUR FUTURE

Grandma used to say: "Children should be seen and not heard." Well we've got news for you...you're no longer a child. If you're going to be more successful, you want to – no – you *need* to, be heard!

Promoting oneself just doesn't seem to be in most people's DNA. It may be because of the way we've been raised or educated, but most people feel uncomfortable singing their own praises. But be aware that, as we've said before, we are each our own brand. We have our own style, our own beliefs, how we think and how we speak. Just as a good product manager will construct a marketing plan for a consumer brand, you need a marketing plan for you which includes when and how you will be heard.

So what does a personal marketing plan look like? First, the message. Put together a brief one-minute "elevator speech" on the critical issues facing your organization, or a project you're working on, or an initiative that you have in mind. Then, think about how you can expand these messages into a full-fledged presentation. Keep these organized messages as close to you as you keep your cell phone.

Now to implementation. One business sage invented the term "managing by walking around." For the moment, we'll call it mobile visibility. Get out of your office and be seen. We knew of someone who would make it a point to stroll the halls on the executive floor just as the monthly board meeting was breaking up hoping to bump into the right people...and another who would ride the elevators at headquarters up and down just before lunch for the same exposure.

While these may seem a bit extreme, they do have a modicum of reason to them.

Beyond mobile visibility, you need to get "bookings"... opportunities to present your thoughts. All organizations, such as companies, associations, academic institutions, clubs, religious groups, etc., have planned venues to communicate to people. These include staff meetings, board meetings, committee meetings, sales conferences, public meetings and other gatherings too numerous to list here. When people get together, they depend on organized communications. And guess what? Lots of people don't like to be in front of a crowd. They would rather be the listener than the speaker. Therefore, these become great booking opportunities for you. Grab the brass ring. Go for it.

Finally, success breeds success. The better you get at clear, concise communications, the more you will be asked to do it. That's the proper implementation of your plan.

An associate of ours, who is technically inclined, spends all of his time in his company's lab. He says that he feels most comfortable there. We called him the other day to see if he had gotten a promotion that he was hoping for. Guess where he was? In the lab. And guess what his answer was? "No."

CHAPTER FIFTY ONE

C FOR YOURSELF

CLARITY, CONCISENESS, COLOR, CONVICTION, CONTROL

Why do interpersonal communications fail so often? It usually isn't for lack of trying. Some people blather on endlessly without enthusiasm, some load as many words and ideas into their messages as they possibly can, others show as much creativity in their messages as they do when they put out their household garbage. And yet others expect their audiences to do all of the work in grasping any semblance of rationale in what they say.

Remember five words that coincidentally (yeah, right) begin with the letter C. These will help you correct communication shortcomings before they happen:

The first is CLARITY. Make your point. As the old brainteaser goes, instead of saying: "It is not efficacious to indoctrinate a superannuated canine with innovative maneuvers." You might try saying: "You can't teach an old dog new tricks." Instead of saying "This project is well conceived and has been based on solid strategic principals known within the industry and has every possibility of succeeding." Say "This project is designed to succeed…and it will."

Next, CONCISENESS, which we will define as saying as much as you need to with as few words as possible. You may have heard the story of the speechwriter who said: "I wrote you a thirty-minute speech because I didn't have time to write you a ten-minute speech." It's hard to make every word and phrase work optimally. Practice "word economy," cut out extraneous language, and keep trimming until all of the fat is gone.

COLOR is the sizzle that sells the steak, the spectrum that attracts us all to rainbows, the flair of the actor playing out a juicy part. Color in the spoken word is a well chosen idiom, a super-interesting anecdote, an unexpected quote, a mind blowing statistic, or a great "word picture." These are all ways to add creativity, interest and originality to a bare bones presentation.

Now to CONVICTION. What made King, Regan and Kennedy great speakers and strong communicators? Yes, they all used the language well, had a good sense of "pacing" and strong non-verbal communication skills. But, most importantly, they all...as do most other good speakers...let their passion and conviction show through. Conviction and passion lead to enthusiasm which leads to success in selling your ideas.

And, finally, CONTROL, an important element both in presenting as well as handling question and answer sessions. When you speak, you need to control the content and the delivery. This is the time to "stick with the script," not a time to innovate or ad lib. In Q&A sessions, control is all about being prepared for the tough questions and repackaging them where you need to. Get off defense and go on offense.

Clarity, conciseness, color, conviction and control...put them all together and you will *Make Your Point!*

Answer to quiz question in Chapter 2: *Where there's smoke, there's fire.*

One more thing...

We're developing our next book. The working concept is *Speakers and Presenters Most Embarrassing Moments*. It's going to be a lighthearted look at those awkward, embarrassing and humorous moments that happen to people before, during or after their presentations. Perhaps you've found yourself in one of those red-faced situations or you've attended a meeting where things just didn't go as the speaker had planned. Or maybe even you witnessed someone in the audience do (or ask) something unforgettably ridiculous. We'd love to hear from you.

Just write-up your story (we suggest between 100 to 200 words) and shoot us an email. Please give your name and address, because if we use your story, we'd like to give you acknowledgment in our book and send you an autographed copy when it comes out. Of course we'll change the names of the people in your story, so don't worry about getting fired when you send us an account of your boss's recent foul up.

Please email your story to: Kevin@kevincarroll.com

Thanks!

Bob & Kevin

Bob Elliott started his career with large corporations including Pfizer, Cigna and Westinghouse. Interested in looking at corporate life from the outside, he became a communications consultant in 1982. Bob is proud of his relationships with America's top companies like GE, MasterCard, and Wal-Mart although at the drop of a hat he will talk about his work with Cindy Crawford and Jimmy Connors.

Bob can be reached at:
12 Coachlamp Lane
Greenwich, CT 06830
203-629-1108
email: Speakcomm@aol.com

Kevin Carroll grew up in a large Irish Catholic family where, to the best of his mother's recollection, he was somewhere near the middle. As one of seven, Kevin learned early on that if you don't make your point, somebody else will make it for you. In 1996, after 17 years in the advertising business, Kevin started his own consulting, speaking and training company. His client roster includes such blue chippers as IBM, Merrill Lynch, Unilever and Cisco Systems.

Kevin can be reached at:
2 Broad Street
Westport, CT 06880
203-226-6493
email: Kevin@kevincarroll.com
website: www.kevincarroll.com

Bob and Kevin speak, train and consult throughout the U.S. and overseas.

Printed in the United States
202233BV00003B/205-255/A

9 781420 804393